WITHDRAWN

No Reading Counts
Or Lexile Information
Available

VIGO COUNTY PUBLIC LIBRARY
TERRE HAUTE, INDIANA

George W. Bush

by Sally Lee

Consulting Editor: Gail Saunders-Smith, PhD

Consultant:
Sheila Blackford
Librarian, Scripps Library
Managing Editor, *American President*
Miller Center, University of Virginia

CAPSTONE PRESS
a capstone imprint

Pebble Plus is published by Capstone Press,
1710 Roe Crest Drive, North Mankato, Minnesota 56003.
www.capstonepub.com

Copyright © 2013 by Capstone Press, a Capstone imprint. All rights reserved.
No part of this publication may be reproduced in whole or in part, or stored in a retrieval system, or transmitted in any form or by any means, electronic, mechanical, photocopying, recording, or otherwise, without written permission of the publisher. For information regarding permission, write to Capstone Press,
1710 Roe Crest Drive, North Mankato, Minnesota 56003.

Library of Congress Cataloging-in-Publication Data
Lee, Sally.
  George W. Bush / by Sally Lee.
    p. cm.—(Pebble plus. Presidential biographies)
  Includes bibliographical references and index.
  Summary: "Simple text and full-color photographs describe the life of George W. Bush"—Provided by publisher.
  ISBN 978-1-4296-8586-3 (library binding)
  ISBN 978-1-62065-318-0 (ebook PDF)
  1. Bush, George W. (George Walker), 1946—Juvenile literature. 2. Presidents—United States—Biography—Juvenile literature. I. Title.
  E903.L44 2013
  973.931092—dc23
  [B]   2011049860

Editorial Credits
Erika L. Shores, editor; Sarah Bennett, designer; Wanda Winch, media researcher; Kathy McColley,
    production specialist

Photo Credits
AP Images: Robert F. Bukaty, 21; Corbis: Sygma/Andrew Lichtenstein, 13; Courtesy of Texas State Library & Archives Commission, 11; Courtesy of the White House: Eric Draper, cover, 1; The George Bush Presidential Library and Museum, 5, 7, 9; The George W. Bush Presidential Library and Museum: White House Photo by Lyndan Steele, 19, White House Photo by Paul Morse, 15, 17

Note to Parents and Teachers

The Presidential Biographies series supports national history standards related to people and culture. This book describes and illustrates the life of George W. Bush. The images support early readers in understanding the text. The repetition of words and phrases helps early readers learn new words. This book also introduces early readers to subject-specific vocabulary words, which are defined in the Glossary section. Early readers may need assistance to read some words and to use the Table of Contents, Glossary, Read More, Internet Sites, and Index sections of the book.

Printed in the United States of America in North Mankato, Minnesota.
052013   007340R

Table of Contents

Early Years

George W. Bush was the
43rd U.S. president. He was born
July 6, 1946, in New Haven,
Connecticut, to Barbara
and George H. W. Bush.
George H. W. Bush was
the 41st U.S. president.

born in
New Haven,
Connecticut

1946

George W. Bush, around age 3

George grew up in Texas.

He was a fun-loving boy

who enjoyed sports,

especially baseball.

He went to a Massachusetts

boarding school for high school.

born in
New Haven,
Connecticut

1946

George played Little League baseball.

Young Adult

George graduated from Yale
and Harvard universities. He trained
as a fighter pilot in the Texas Air
National Guard. Later, George
started his own oil company
in Midland, Texas. In 1977
he married Laura Welch.

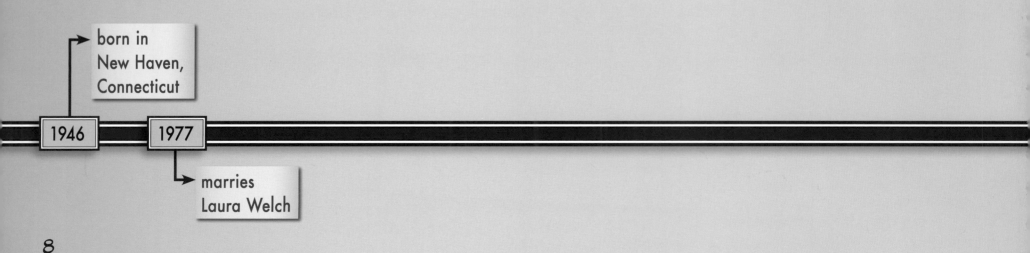

born in
New Haven,
Connecticut

1946

1977

marries
Laura Welch

George, Laura, and their twin daughters, Jenna (left) and Barbara (right), in 1990

Life in Texas

In 1988 George helped run his father's presidential campaign. In 1989 he became part owner of the Texas Rangers baseball team. He won his first political office when he was elected governor of Texas in 1994.

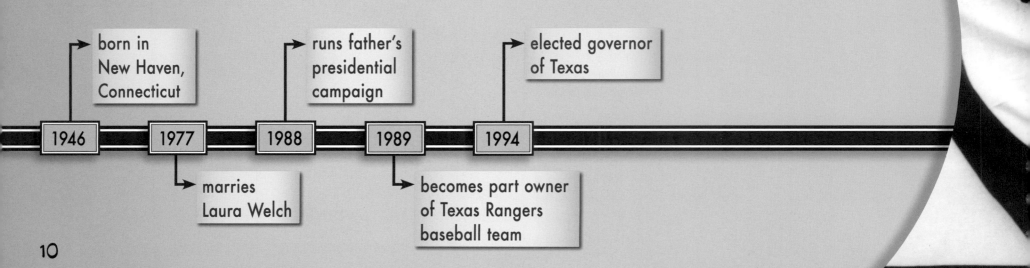

born in
New Haven,
Connecticut

runs father's
presidential
campaign

elected governor
of Texas

1946   1977   1988   1989   1994

marries
Laura Welch

becomes part owner
of Texas Rangers
baseball team

George was a popular governor
who listened to everyone's ideas.
He used more state money for
schools and improved education.
After six years as governor,
he ran for U.S. president.

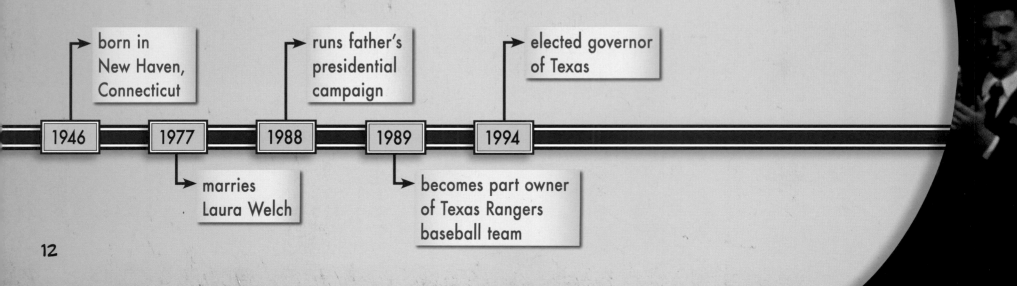

born in
New Haven,
Connecticut

runs father's
presidential
campaign

elected governor
of Texas

1946   1977   1988   1989   1994

marries
Laura Welch

becomes part owner
of Texas Rangers
baseball team

President Bush

George became president

on January 20, 2001.

He passed laws to help

more children succeed in school.

He also lowered taxes.

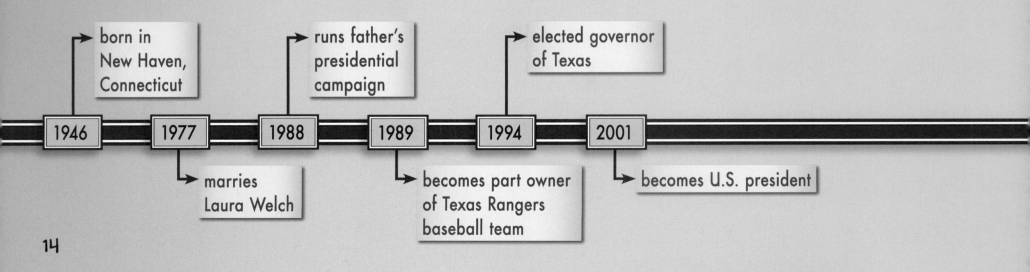

born in
New Haven,
Connecticut

runs father's
presidential
campaign

elected governor
of Texas

1946   1977   1988   1989   1994   2001

marries
Laura Welch

becomes part owner
of Texas Rangers
baseball team

becomes U.S. president

No Child Left Behind

On September 11, 2001, terrorists attacked the United States. Nearly 3,000 people were killed. George worked hard to prevent more attacks. He sent the military to Afghanistan to destroy terrorist groups.

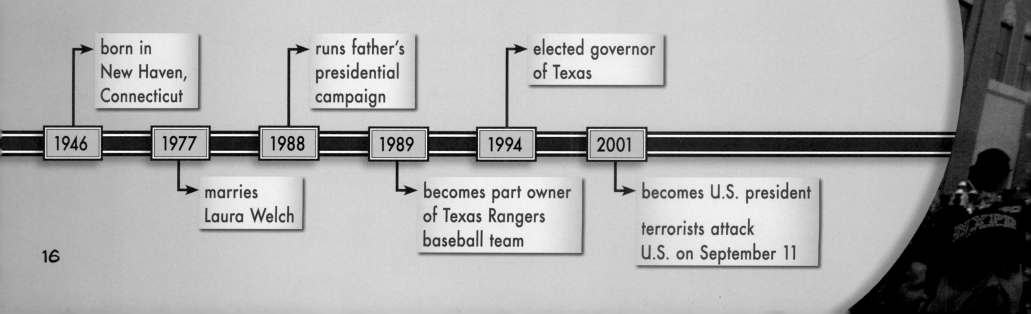

| 1946 | 1977 | 1988 | 1989 | 1994 | 2001 |

born in New Haven, Connecticut

runs father's presidential campaign

elected governor of Texas

marries Laura Welch

becomes part owner of Texas Rangers baseball team

becomes U.S. president

terrorists attack U.S. on September 11

George believed the country
of Iraq was hiding weapons.
He didn't trust Iraq's leader,
Saddam Hussein. In 2003
George gave the orders
to invade Iraq.

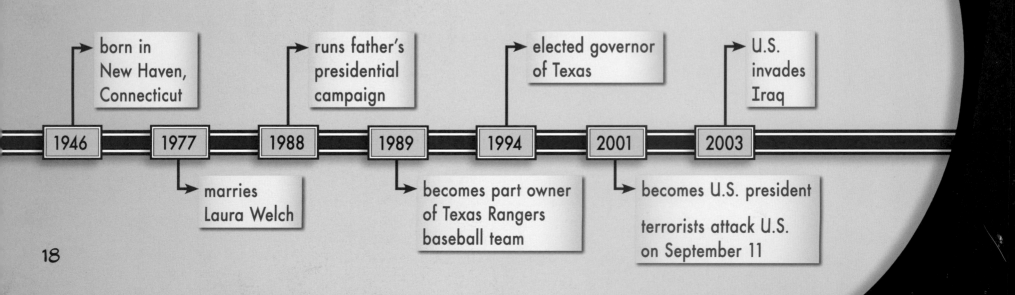

born in
New Haven,
Connecticut

runs father's
presidential
campaign

elected governor
of Texas

U.S.
invades
Iraq

1946   1977   1988   1989   1994   2001   2003

marries
Laura Welch

becomes part owner
of Texas Rangers
baseball team

becomes U.S. president

terrorists attack U.S.
on September 11

George left office in 2009
after eight years as president.
People will always remember
how he helped the nation
through its worst terrorist attack.

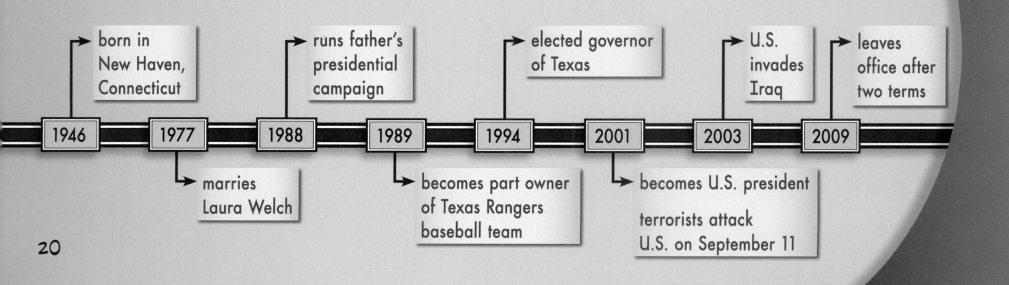

born in
New Haven,
Connecticut

runs father's
presidential
campaign

elected governor
of Texas

U.S.
invades
Iraq

leaves
office after
two terms

| 1946 | 1977 | 1988 | 1989 | 1994 | 2001 | 2003 | 2009 |

marries
Laura Welch

becomes part owner
of Texas Rangers
baseball team

becomes U.S. president

terrorists attack
U.S. on September 11

Glossary

boarding school—a school that students live at during the school year

campaign—a contest between people who are running for a political office

invade—to enter or attack as an enemy

military—the armed forces, including the Army, Navy, Air Force, Marines, and Coast Guard

political—the work or study of government

tax—money that people or businesses must give to the government to pay for what the government does

terrorist—a person who uses harmful acts and fear to get what they want

university—a large school that a student may attend after high school

Read More

Lee, Sally. *Laura Bush*. First Ladies. Mankato, Minn.: Capstone Press, 2011.

Rumsch, BreAnn. *George W. Bush*. The United States Presidents. Ecina, Minn.: ABDO Pub. Co., 2009.

Venezia, Mike. *George W. Bush: Forty-Third President, 2001–Present*. Getting to Know the U.S. Presidents. New York: Children's Press/Scholastic, 2008.

Internet Sites

FactHound offers a safe, fun way to find Internet sites related to this book. All of the sites on FactHound have been researched by our staff.

Here's all you do:

Visit *www.facthound.com*

Type in this code: 9781429685863

Super-cool stuff!

Check out projects, games and lots more at
www.capstonekids.com

Index

Word Count: 261

Grade: 1

Early-Intervention Level: 21